Start with Sport and Leisure

© Aladdin Books Ltd 2000

Designed and produced by
Aladdin Books Ltd
28 Percy Street
London W1P 0LD

ISBN 0 7496 3766 8 (hardcover)
ISBN 0 7496 4617 9 (paperback)

First published in Great Britain
in 2000 by
Franklin Watts
96 Leonard Street
London EC2A 4XD

Project Editor
Sally Hewitt

Editor
Liz White

Designer
Flick Killerby

Illustrator
Catherine Ward - SGA

Picture Research
Brooks Krikler Research

Printed in the U.A.E.
All rights reserved

Original Design Concept
David West Children's Books

A CIP catalogue entry for this book is available from the British Library.

The project editor, Sally Hewitt, is an experienced teacher. She writes and edits books for children on a wide variety of subjects including art, music, science and maths.

The author, Sue Lacey, is an experienced teacher of art. She currently teaches primary school children in the south of England. In her spare time, she paints and sculpts.

photocredits: Abbreviations: t-top, m-middle, b-bottom, r-right, l-left, c-centre
Pages 4, 7, 11, 13, 15, 16, 19, 20, 23, 27 & 29 - AKG London. 24 - The Musée Picasso, Paris © Succession Picasso / DACS 2000. 30 AKG©Salvador Dali - Foundation Gala-Salvador Dali / DACS 2000.

The publishers have made every effort to contact all the relevant copyright holders and apologise for any omissions that may have inadvertently been made.

Start with Art

Sport and Leisure

Sue Lacey

FRANKLIN WATTS
LONDON • SYDNEY

INTRODUCTION

Artists work with many different tools and materials to make art. They also spend a great deal of time looking carefully at patterns, shapes and colours.

This book is about how artists see **sport and leisure**. In the past, before television, computers and cinema, people had very different ways of spending their leisure time. They would go on picnics, sit in cafés, or perhaps go on boating trips. You can see this in their paintings.

You don't have to be a brilliant artist to do the projects in this book, just have fun being creative.

CONTENTS

WORKING LIKE AN ARTIST PAGES 6–7
Learn how to work like a true artist. Use a sketch book and collect ideas from around you. Read the tips on how to draw people in action.

MACKE PAGES 8-9
Watercolour picnic Macke painted a scene in shades of blue. Try using inks to make your own scene.

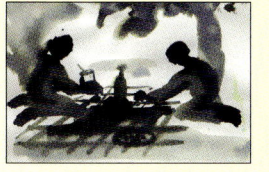

MÜNTER PAGES 10-11
Expressionist boat trip Münter used simple shapes and colours. Try making a collage using her style.

GREEK POTTERY PAGES 12-13
Ancient Greek art The ancient Greeks would often decorate pottery. This one has a sporting scene. Try making your own Greek vase.

TENNIS ETCHING PAGES 14-15
Etching Have a look at this old style tennis print. You can make one with inks and polystyrene.

BRUEGHEL PAGES 16-17
Detailed ice skaters Brueghel painted a winter sporting scene in detail. You can make a snowy collage.

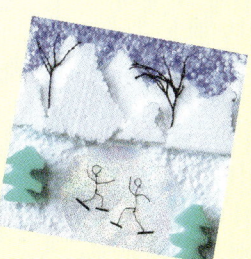

DEGAS PAGES 18-19
3-D ballet dancers Degas painted and sculpted some wonderful ballet dancers. Make your own 3-D sporting figure.

SEURAT PAGES 20-21
Pointillist circus Seurat painted a pointillist circus scene, using lots of different coloured dots. Try to make a mobile using the same technique.

INDIAN MOGHUL STYLE PAGES 22-23

Miniature painting Long ago people painted small pictures on paper, wood or fabric. You can create your very own Indian-style miniature painting.

PICASSO PAGES 24-25
Abstract ball player Picasso used some strange shapes. Look at the shapes in Picasso's painting. What sport is being played?

RENOIR PAGES 26-27

Street scene in oils Renoir used oils to paint a dancing scene. You can use oil pastels to create the same effect.

GAUGUIN PAGES 28-29
Painted horse riders Gauguin painted horse riders galloping along the beach. You can make a 3-D scene of horses and riders.

DALI PAGES 30-31
Surrealist footballer Like Dali you can make your own surrealist sportsperson. You could make a footballer, cricketer, netball player or tennis player.

GLOSSARY/INDEX PAGE 32

WORKING LIKE AN ARTIST

It can help you in your work if you start by looking carefully and collecting ideas, just like an artist. Artists usually carry a sketch book round with them all the time so they can get their ideas on paper straight away.

Words
You can write some words to remind you of the shapes, colours and patterns you see.

Materials
Try out different pencils, pens, paints, pastels, crayons and materials to see what they do. Which would be the best for this work?

Colour
When using colour, mix all the colours you want first and try them out. It is amazing how many different colours you can make.

Using a sketch book Before you start each project, this is the place to do your sketches. Try out your tools and materials, mix colours and stick in some interesting papers and fabrics. You can then choose which you want to use.

Be a magpie
Make a collection of things that are of interest to you like feathers, stones or materials. Anything that catches your eye could be useful in your artwork.

Art box You can collect tools and materials together for your work and put them in a box. Sometimes you may need to go to an art shop to buy exactly what you need. Often you can find things at home you can use. Ask for something for your art box for your birthday!

Drawing sporting figures

It can seem difficult to draw people in action, but if you take your time, do some sketches and look carefully, you can do it!

Body shapes
Start by drawing simple shapes to show the head, arms and legs. Look at how the body is made up.

Try to break the body down into easy lines. Think of the shoulders as one line, the arms and legs as others.

Make sure you have made the head the right size, and check that the legs are not too long or too short.

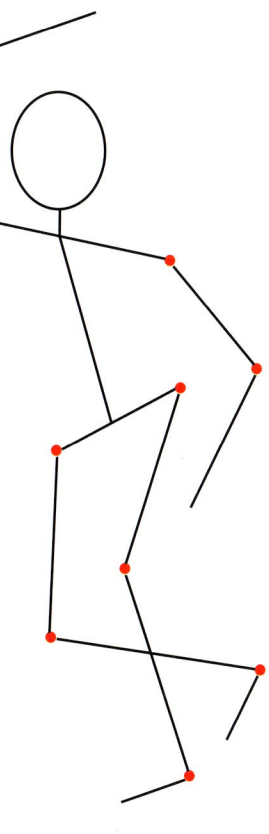

Look at where the joints are and how they move.

Once you have mastered this and the proportions look right, try drawing a different pose using the same technique.

WHAT YOU NEED
Thick white paper
Indian ink
Water
Sketch book
Paintbrush

WATERCOLOUR PICNIC

By adding different amounts of water to one colour, August Macke could paint using different shades of blue. Why not try using inks to paint a picnic picture? Add different amounts of water to the colour you choose to make different tones.

Project: Painting with ink

Step 1. Make a sketch of a picnic scene on thick white paper. In your sketch book, mix some indian ink with water to make three tones of the same colour - dark, medium and light.

Step 2. Starting with the light tone, paint in the shapes. While the ink is still wet, paint in the medium and dark tones.

Gallery

The Picnic After Sailing 1913
August Macke (1887-1914)

Watercolours
Macke usually painted in bright oil paints, but he was also skilled with watercolours.

Picnic
Many artists at this time painted picnic scenes.

Shades
How many different shades of blue can you see in this painting?

Colour
The boat tells us that this was a river picnic and could be the reason Macke chose watery colours.

Although the German artist August Macke was a good student, he left school to become a painter before taking his final exams. He soon met other famous artists who decided to paint using colours full of feeling. When he died in 1914, during the First World War, his friend Marc said, "With the loss of his harmony of colours German art will become paler."

Expressionist boat trip

WHAT YOU NEED
Selection of papers and card • Fabrics
Pencil • Paper
Scissors • Glue

The colours and shapes used by Gabriele Münter are very pleasing to the eye and can easily be turned into a collage. If you draw, cut and stick some simple shapes cut from card or fabrics, you can make a boating scene of your own.

Project: **Boating collage**

Step 1. Draw your picture of a boating scene onto card using simple shapes. Collect different papers and fabrics that are good colours for your scene.

Step 2. Cut out mountains, fields and water shapes for the background and water. Arrange them on the card. Add a boat and people.

Step 3. When you are happy with the arrangement, stick everything down with glue.

Gallery

Boat Trip 1910
Gabriele Münter (1877-1962)

People
A group of Expressionist artists used to go on holiday together each year to paint. Could this be the artists on a boat trip?

Composition
The arrangement of people, background colours and shapes cleverly draws your eye round the picture.

Shape
Münter liked to change what she saw into simpler shapes and colours.

Feeling
How does this picture make you feel? Do you think Münter liked boating trips?

When Gabriele Münter started painting in Germany, women were not allowed to put their pictures into art exhibitions with men. They were expected to stay at home and look after their families. But Gabriele spent her life painting. She particularly liked painting people. She said her work was about self-expression and she became a member of the Expressionist group of painters.

ANCIENT GREEK ART

WHAT YOU NEED
Glass or plastic kitchen bowl
Cling film • Paints
Newspaper
Flour • Water
Paintbrush • Glue
Card • Scissors

Pottery in ancient Greek times was made by specially trained potters who were very skilled in using clay. Pots and bowls can be made out of papier mâché too, so follow the instructions and try it for yourself!

PROJECT: **PAPIER MÂCHÉ BOWL**

Step 1. Ask if you may use a glass or plastic kitchen bowl and line it with cling film.

Step 2. Mix flour and water to make a soggy paste. Tear up newspaper strips, dip them into the paste and use them to layer onto the inside of the dish.

Step 3. Make five or six layers leaving the papier mâché to dry between layers. When it is all dry, lift the paper bowl out carefully. Add handles.

Step 4. Paint your bowl black or blue on the outside and terracotta red inside. Cut out some athletes from orange card or paper and stick them round the pot.

Gallery

Greek Red-Figure Vase c510/500 B.C.
Ancient Greece

Olympics
Greek men and women enjoyed athletics and held the first Olympic Games. Many vases showed athletes taking part in games.

Background
The black background of the pot was painted with a special clay which turned black when heated.

Use
What do you think this vase was used for?

This is a picture from a vase made by a Greek potter long ago. The potter would make the vase or bowl out of red clay. He would then paint the pottery with a liquid clay and draw figures onto the surface using a sharp tool. The heat of the kiln turned the liquid clay black and the figures would stay red like the clay.

WHAT YOU NEED
Pencil • Paper
Polystyrene sheet
Biro • Ink
Paintbrush
Thick paper

ETCHING

Making an etching can be quite dangerous because chemicals are used. It is much safer to use a polystyrene press print sheet, which can make a very effective print.

PROJECT: TENNIS PRINT

Step 1. Do a drawing of a tennis game. Use simple shapes and lines. Copy it onto the polystyrene sheet.

Step 2. Use a biro or blunt pencil to press into the drawing on the sheet to make lines. To make the shape of a tennis dress or shorts ask an adult to cut away these areas.

Step 3. Choose a coloured ink and paint it onto the surface of the polystyrene. Press a thick piece of paper onto the ink and peel it off.

14

Gallery

Le Jeu de Paume 1750
Tennis Etching

Costume
Would you like to play tennis in these clothes? The clothing gives you a clue about the date of this tennis game.

Fine Lines
Many fine lines have been drawn close to each other to show shadows. This is called cross-hatching.

Colour
As this is a print, only a few colours have been used. Can you see what they are?

History
You can learn a great deal about the past by looking carefully at a work of art like this and comparing it with life today.

Illustrations for books were often made by etching. The artist would draw a detailed picture onto a sheet of metal and use acid to burn into the metal along the lines. Colours would then be put on the metal sheet. Sometimes the artist would add colour or blacker lines after the print had been made.

Detailed ice skaters

WHAT YOU NEED
Blunt knife • Paints
Polystyrene • Glue
Felt-tip pen • Sponge
Shiny paper • Twigs
Wire / Pipe cleaners
Used matchstick
Paintbrush

Pieter Brueghel was one of a large family of painters. He often painted cool, wintery scenes with people enjoying the ice and snow. Look for some packaging materials that could make a collage of a snowy scene. Make sure they are cool colours.

Gallery

Winter 1622-1635
Pieter Brueghel (1564-1638)

Distance
The people in the front (foreground) are much bigger than those in the distance. Yet they are all carefully painted.

Activities
How many different activities can you see going on? Did you spot a man who had fallen into the river?

In Holland during the winter, when the canals and rivers had frozen over, people enjoyed skating on them. Pieter Brueghel painted many scenes of children and adults spending time together having fun.

Project: Snow and Ice Collage

Step 1. Ask an adult to help you to cut out a square from polystyrene packaging and draw mountains and a lake area on it in felt pen.

Step 2. Get an adult to help you cut away the polystyrene to make the mountains and lake shapes. Use a blunt knife very carefully. Paint the sky blue and add some of the cut-out mountain shapes to make more mountains. Stick on a piece of shiny paper for a pond.

Step 3. The figures can be made from wire or pipe cleaners. Add skates to the feet by painting a used matchstick black. Ask an adult to cut it in four. Green sponge and twigs will make trees. Glue everything on to complete your picture.

3-D BALLET DANCERS

WHAT YOU NEED
Thick card
Pencil • Scissors
Paint • Paintbrush
Needle • Cotton
Netting

Degas made many paintings and sculptures of ballet dancers. This sculpture is full of life although it is made of metal. The same lively feeling can be given to a 3-D model made out of card.

Project: 3-D figures

Step 1. Draw a figure onto thick card. You may need some help to cut it out. Degas chose a ballet dancer, but you can choose any sport.

Step 2. Paint both sides of your figure. If you chose a dancer, sew a line of stitches along the top of a small piece of netting and tie it around the waist.

Step 3. Make a base by cutting halfway through two pieces of card and slotting them together.

Step 4. Make a cut between your figure's feet. Slot your figure into the stand. You could make a whole troupe or team.

Gallery

Dancer 1896-1911
Edgar Degas (1834-1917)

Clay
First Degas made a ballet dancer from clay, it was then cast in bronze.

Lifelike
The final bronze dancer looks almost alive!

Bronze
This ballet dancer is made from bronze, which is a metal. It starts as a liquid and is poured into a mould of the sculpture. When it is solid it is polished until it shines.

Edgar Degas loved to go behind the scenes at the Paris theatres to watch the ballet dancers. He would take his sketchbook, pastels, pencils and paints and make sketches. When he returned to his studio he would turn his sketches into beautiful sculptures and paintings.

Pointillist circus

WHAT YOU NEED
Coloured card
Pencil • Scissors
Tracing paper
Felt-tip pens
Cotton
Garden stick

The circus figures look as though they could be attached to the top of the tent by wires. A group of circus figures hanging on threads would make a moving mobile. It could look good hanging up in your bedroom.

Gallery

Le Cirque 1891
Georges Seurat (1859-1891)

White
The white horse and edge of the ring are the first things you look at.

Curves
The curved line takes your eye round the painting and makes you feel as if you are in a circus ring.

Coloured dots
From a distance it is hard to see all the dots Seurat used, but if you look closely you can see each coloured dot.

Project: Circus mobile

Step 1. Copy the circus figures from Seurat's painting onto coloured card. You could enlarge them on a photocopier and trace them. When your figures are finished, cut them out.

Georges Seurat trained as an artist in Paris. He tried different methods of painting, but is most famous for his style called pointillism. You can see how he put dots of colour next to each other in this picture of the circus. He spent a long time arranging different coloured dots to see the effect they had and the different colours they made, before he painted his pictures.

Step 2. Use felt-tip pens to put dots of colour all over both sides of the figures. Experiment with combining dots of different colours to see what new colours you can make.

Step 3. Tie threads of different lengths onto each figure and then tie them onto a garden stick. Add a long thread to the stick and hang it up in your room.

MINIATURE PAINTING

WHAT YOU NEED
White fabric
Board • Pencil
Fabric paints
Ink • Thick paintbrush
Thin paintbrush
Sequins • Glue

Indian artists painted small pictures which usually told a story. They painted them on paper, wood, ivory or fabric. Today, there are many different types of fabric paints and crayons which can be used to make a picture.

PROJECT: PAINTING FABRIC

Step 1. Find a small square of white fabric. Pin it to a piece of board and sketch your picture with pencil. You could use the Moghul painting as a guide.

Step 2. Colour your drawing by using fabric paints or inks. Colour in the main areas first, using a thick brush.

Step 3. Use a fine brush for the details. Paint a frame around the edge and glue sequins to decorate it when it is dry.

Gallery

Prince with Falcon
Moghul Style (Beg. 17th Century)

Sport
What sport do you think is illustrated here? The bird is a clue.

Colour
The man in the painting is a prince. He stands out in his brightly coloured clothes.

Illustration
This painting could have been done to illustrate a book about life in the Emperor's court.

Miniature
Paintings like this were often very small. Fine brushes of animal hair would be used to paint the delicate lines.

Long ago in Northern India, artists painted pictures of everyday life at the Emperor's court. Often these were miniatures, which means the paintings were very small. The artist would tell a story in paint about important events like elephants escaping or royal hunting expeditions.

Abstract Ball Player

WHAT YOU NEED
Paper • Fine pen
Heavier pen
Coloured pens

Picasso used all sorts of weird and wonderful shapes in his paintings. He did not paint realistic pictures that showed exactly what things looked like. You can make a Picasso-style painting by finding shapes in scribbles!

Gallery

Ball Players on the Beach 1928
Pablo Picasso (1881-1973)

Shapes
Look at the person drawn in black in the background. How is this one different in shape to the main person painted?

Body
Look at the person playing with the ball. Can you work out which bits are arms and legs?

Project: Finding shapes

Step 1. Make some scribbles on a piece of paper using a fine pen. Take some time to look at the shapes you have made. Can you see shapes that could be made into figures or balls?

The Spanish artist Pablo Picasso changed how people saw art in the last century. He created paintings, sculptures, drawings and ceramics which were all unusual or different to the work of other artists at that time. He used his imagination because he did not want his art to be realistic, like a photograph. When you look at one of his paintings it may take you some time to work out what some of the things in them are!

Step 2. Draw over your figure in a heavier pen. You could also colour it in following the lines of the scribbles.

Street scene in oils

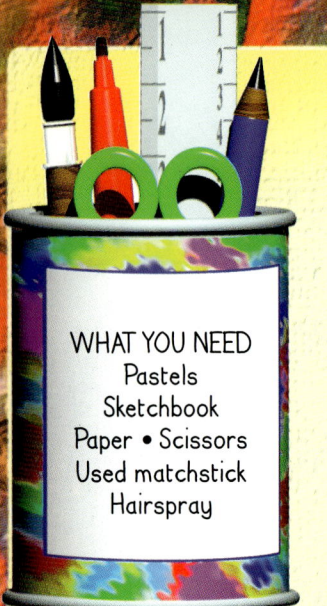

WHAT YOU NEED
Pastels
Sketchbook
Paper • Scissors
Used matchstick
Hairspray

Renoir used oil paints for this picture of his friends enjoying a day away from work. Pastels are also effective when drawing people. Why not try drawing some Parisian dancers as Renoir has done, or some of your friends at a disco?

Project: Pastel dancers

Step 1. Test out your pastels in a sketchbook first to see how you can layer them or blend them. Draw a picture of people dancing. Fill in the background with different pastel shades.

Step 2. Colour in the dancers. To get the effect of dappled light on the picture, scrape off some of the oil pastel using a used matchstick.

Step 3. Trim your picture and spray it with hairspray to prevent smudging.

Gallery

The Ball at the Moulin de la Galette 1876
Pierre Auguste Renoir (1841-1919)

Costume
Renoir has caught the spirit of the time by showing the details of the clothes. The hats and dresses show how Parisians dressed for a ball in 1876.

Street Life
The people of Paris loved to spend their time outside in parks and squares. Here they are talking, eating and dancing.

Light
The light seems to be coming through the trees. Renoir has used a light-coloured oil paint to show the effect of sunlight.

Many of Pierre Auguste Renoir's paintings show people enjoying themselves. He began work at the age of 13 and spent his entire life painting the people and places he knew. The use of bright, fresh colours brought a cheerful touch to his work. He spent time with Monet painting outside and studying the effect of sunlight. During his lifetime Renoir became world famous. Today, people still travel all over the world to see his paintings.

Painted Horse Riders

WHAT YOU NEED
Stiff card
Paint • Paintbrushes
Pencils • Scissors
Card • Glue

Many people enjoy riding along the beach like the figures in Gauguin's painting. They almost look as though they could jump out of the back of the picture. A 3-D effect can be achieved by cutting out horses and riders and adding them to a background.

Project: 3-D horse riders

Step 1. Paint a beach background onto stiff card. Draw some horses and riders onto another piece of card. Paint them in warm colours. Use Gauguin's picture to help you choose shapes and colours.

Step 2. Cut out the horses and riders and stick a piece of folded zig-zag card onto the back of each.

Step 3. Glue the other end of the zig-zag to the background to finish the picture.

Gallery

Riders on the Beach 1902
Paul Gauguin (1848-1903)

Time of Day
The warm but soft colours could be the early morning or evening light on the beach.

Freedom
The figures are not wearing many clothes and are riding their horses bareback.

Brush Strokes
Gauguin has used different kinds of brush strokes to blend colours together for the sky, sea and sand.

Feeling
How does the painting make you feel? How do you think Gauguin felt when he painted it?

Paul Gauguin was born in Paris. However he left his family and career in France to spend much of his life on the South Sea island of Tahiti. He hated city life and enjoyed living a simple life close to nature. Many of his paintings were of the tropical forests and beaches where he loved the freedom of riding a horse. The warm colours he used show the enjoyment he had in his way of life.

WHAT YOU NEED
Pencil • Scissors
Thick coloured card
Tape • Cotton
Paper fasteners

SURREALIST FOOTBALLER

It is easy to turn a two-dimensional drawing into a movable figure if you use Salvador Dali's unusual footballer to help you. Look closely at Dali's drawing, then draw the athlete of your choice and make a heart shape at the centre.

GALLERY

Football Player c.1980
SALVADOR DALI (1904-1989)

SKELETON
This footballer has no skin or face and is not at all like a real football player.

LAYERS
It is as if Dali has got under the skin of the footballer to see his movements and feelings.

CENTRE
What shape has been used to frame the football at the centre of the figure? What do you think it means?

DRAWING
You can see how skilled Dali was at drawing from the detailed skeleton.

Project: Movable Figure

Step 1. Draw a head and body on thick coloured card. Cut out a heart shape from the chest. Tape the heart shape onto the side of the heart like a little door. Ask an adult to make holes as shown.

Step 2. Cut out two sets of arms and legs as shown above and ask an adult to make holes as shown. Fix your figure together using paper fasteners so that it moves.

After working in the USA for a number of years, Salvador Dali returned to Spain where he had been born. He was a member of the Surrealist movement of artists. His art work was famous because he painted people, places and objects in great detail, putting them together into a picture in an unusual way.

Step 3. Draw something related to your favourite sport that is small enough to hang onto a piece of cotton in the heart shape in your figure.

GLOSSARY

ABSTRACT Shapes and patterns grouped together to make a picture.

COLLAGE Placing different materials onto a background to make a pattern or picture.

ETCHING Acid is used to cut out a picture into a piece of metal. Ink is then put on and a print made of it.

EXPRESSIONISM A style of art that uses colour, line and shape to show emotion rather than to make pictures that look like the real world.

FOREGROUND The part of the view that is in the front of a picture.

MODEL A smaller than life three-dimensional sculpture of an animal, person or object.

POINTILLISM Dots of paint put close to each other which the eye turns into blocks of colour.

REALISTIC A work of art that is made to look exactly like the real world.

SCULPTURE Making shapes from hard or soft materials, to make a person, animal or design that can be looked at from all sides.

SURREALISM Art that brings together unusual objects and imaginary places that would not be seen in the real world.

THREE-DIMENSIONAL Sometimes shortened to 3-D. An object or work of art that you can walk all around and look at from all sides.

TONES The many different shades or tints of a colour.

INDEX

A
abstract 24, 32

B
background 10, 11, 28
bronze 19

C
clay 12, 13, 19
collage 5, 10, 16, 17, 32
costume 27
crayons 22

E
etching 5, 14, 32
expressionism 5, 11, 32

F
fabrics 5, 6, 10, 22
foreground 16, 32

I
imagination 25
ink 5, 8, 14, 22, 32

M
miniatures 5, 22, 23
mobile 5, 20, 21
model 19, 32

O
oil paints 9, 26, 27

P
papier mâché 12

pastels 19, 26
pointillism 5, 20, 21, 32
pottery 5, 12, 13

R
realistic 24, 25, 32

S
sculpture 5, 18, 19, 25, 32
surrealism 5, 30, 31, 32

T
three-dimensional 5, 18, 28, 32
tones 8, 32

W
watercolour 9